Art Textiles of the World

JAPAN

volume 2

TELOS

Contents

left:
Suzumi Noda
Word Work Diet T-shirt
2000
printed and knitted cotton cloth

Introduction

In recent years, Japanese textile art has forged ahead with new artists emerging one after another. In the 1970's and 80's, the number of Japanese artists working on the international stage increased and in the 1990's exhibitions introducing work in this field increased both inside and outside Japan.

The gloom that surrounds the Japanese economy since the latter half of the 1990's, however, has had an inevitable effect on the world of fine art. Many companies have withdrawn support for cultural activities, and some galleries supported by corporate sponsorship closed and with them exhibitions of textile art disappeared. Kyoto's International Textile Competition, which drew attention from around the world, was last staged in 1999 with no prospect of another one. In spite of these conditions, groups of artists have continued to hold private exhibitions and, by actively participating in exhibitions held overseas, have been able to show their work. The world of Japanese textiles (fiber art) has emerged from the dialogue between the traditions of Japanese dyeing and weaving, and the innovative use of space in a way that is unique to Japanese culture. Recently, a new breed of artists, one deeply rooted in Japanese society and with a social message, has been gaining attention.

Kyoko Kumai, who took an early interest in using stainless steel, incorporates concepts from nature such as wind and light in her work. Shihoko Fukumoto, who creates works that express the relationship between the blues of *aizome* (indigo dyeing) and fabric, has been regularly featured in international exhibitions since the time when Japanese artists were concentrating on natural materials in their work. Hisako Sekijima introduced a new world of basketry to Japan. She learned this expression while living in America and has exhibited examples of baskets never before seen in traditional Japanese *kago* (baskets).

Hisako Sekijima
Difference

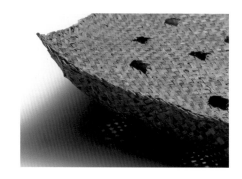

Tetsuo Fujimoto moved from his unique use of double layered textiles to machine embroidery techniques, and was thus able to express 'macro' and 'micro' worlds in fabric, winning the Grand Prix in the 1999 International Textile Competition. Hiroko Ohte employs double weave techniques, draping weighty, richly colored cloths in space. Recently, however, she has begun using more subdued shades in her work. Noriko Narahira incorporates machine stitching she learned in England into her work. She has been selected for several exhibitions including the International Lace Biennale in Belgium, where her entries were awarded prizes. She is now developing her own unique vision.

Jun Mitsuhashi
Moon Ship

Takehiko Sanada, Tsuguo Yanai, and Chika Ohgi are concentrating on work with natural materials. Sanada, who once worked in the world of fashion, has recently been creating works that bring out the tactile qualities of wool.

Yanai and Ohgi focus on the use Japanese paper. Yanai uses paper to produce large-scale works. Ohgi has learned traditional *washi* (Japanese paper) techniques. She creates installations, using paper she has made herself, where space itself is an essential element of the work.

Other artists working with the concept of space include Yuka Kawai, Koji Takaki, and Jun Mitsuhashi. Kawai uses weaving and pleating techniques, and whilst Takaki expresses his ideas through machine stitching and fraying, they both work with the notion of space. In his early work, Mitsuhashi expressed his ideas by means of flat dyed surfaces, but he is now producing works that combine various materials and make greater use of space.

In this new volume, it is perhaps Reiko Sudo and Suzumi Noda who best represent the new type of artist working with textiles. Sudo is exploring the possibilities for the fabric known as *nuno* (cloth), developing new fabrics using traditional dyeing and weaving methods, as well as computers and the latest technology. Noda uses cloth printed with computer-generated text to construct her work, adding another layer of meaning to the incisive messages on Japanese society, which her installations convey. There is a trend to regard artists like Noda, who is involved in both mixed media and fashion, concentrating on fabric as a material for her work, as the most contemporary 'textile artists'. The world of modern textiles (fiber art) in Japan has, until now, been articulated in terms of the space in which works will be exhibited and the connection with natural materials.

A new age is dawning, carrying forward ideas which have their roots in the world of IT (Interface Technology). Given the current state of flux in both the world of technology and of art the possibilities are infinite and it is hard to see precisely in which direction these ideas will end up taking us. In the past, textiles based on traditional Japanese designs (techniques and aesthetics) have gained critical acclaim overseas. Bearing this in mind, it will be very interesting to see how the creation of a fresh identity for Japanese art textiles, less reliant on the past, will be received outside Japan.

Keiko Kawashima
Director
Kyoto International Contemporary
Textile Art Centre (KICTAC)
and Gallery Gallery, Kyoto

Becoming Japanese:
The Birth of an Art Movement

Not many years ago one travelled the earth in search of the Other. Today one travels across continents to see the same suite of photographs, an identical installation, or another interchangeable video. International curators gather the work of a small cannon of artists in Korea and Turkey, in Brazil and Germany, in the United States and Japan. The Other seems to have lost out to globalization, to intellectualization, to artists seeking a place in the same sun, over and over again.

But here and there, despite the overbearing influence of the Art World, small movements in disparate countries shine quietly and brilliantly alone. Contemporary art in Spain remains stubbornly Spanish. To visit ARCO, the mid-winter art fair in Madrid, is to watch Spaniards buying their own paintings – the international crowd notably missing. For here, work by unknown artists resonates as deeply Spanish: art born of the Spanish soil and washed with the darker presence of the Spanish Mediterranean sun with its reds and browns, its ochres and blacks. It seems as though Antoni Tàpies, born in 1923 in Catalonia, located in the ancient Romanesque culture around him the elements that have come to define the essence of Spain in the art of this time. Simplicity, rigor, and clarity of form, combined with an unerring sense of scale. These he transformed into paintings, constructions, and graphic work.

During the 1980s German painting caught international attention. It was bold – brutal even, aggressive, full of confident gesture and brilliant color. This art seemed to have erupted from the German psyche. These Germanic neo-expressionists dominated exhibitions around the globe, found their counterparts in American painting, became hot, and then slipped into the background, replaced by the installation art of the 1990s, which in turn would be replaced a few years later by video.

Contemporary Japanese fiber art is still another story. A few years ago the exhibition 'Japanese Art After 1945' opened in New York's Guggenheim Museum. Janet Koplos, Senior Editor for *Art in America* was writing about the show and, troubled, she called me. Koplos knew I had recently organized a three-part exhibition in North Dakota, 'Light and Shadow: Japanese Artists in Space.'

Koji Takaki
Ma (detail)

Would I come by her office after seeing the Guggenheim exhibition?

As I walked quickly through the show, I understood. Once again, the international art community had curated the exhibition. Glaringly missing were contemporary fiber artists and what they represent – just as no Spanish painters appear in the international biennials.

Japanese fiber artists accomplished a rare thing in the last decades of the twentieth century. They went out into the world, assessed the textile field, competed in the big fiber exhibitions, and went home to create an art movement that is truly their own. In this they echo their ancestors who over the years have taken the discoveries of other peoples and turned them into something truly Japanese.

Shihoko
Fukumoto
Hikari No Yukue

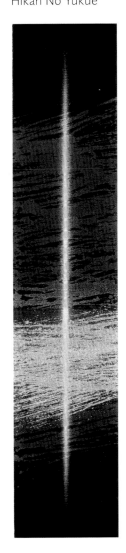

Their assessment took place during the glory years of the Lausanne Tapestry Biennials. The history of those Swiss exhibitions is legend. Established in 1962 to bring international attention to works woven on high or low looms, that is tapestries, it wasn't long before participating artists foiled the exhibition founders and nudged the rules aside. Both embroidery and appliqué were accepted into the second biennial and the third allowed an undefined experimental section. With gleeful abandon, artists integrated contemporary ideas about art into the realm of tapestry. They invented new techniques and adapted old ones to fresh uses. They appropriated materials from both industry and the town dump, from troves of historical textiles and the halls of modern industrial design. And they expanded the function of "tapestry" to encompass all of space.

In 1981, the organizers of the tenth biennial proposed a survey of the newly evolving textile arts. Clearly, tapestry had been replaced by experimentation. There was also a gentle but persistent breeze blowing in from the far Pacific as Japanese artists brought their own sensibility, coupled with their sophisticated dyeing techniques, into the contemporary textile field. More often than not, the exhibition labels describing the work of Japanese artists read "own technique."

For truly, these were years of experimentation for Japanese fiber artists. Some, investigating European traditions, created heavy, bold work – decidedly non-Asian – even though their own heritage did not embrace woven wool tapestries intended to adorn walls. Those early European-style wall hangings easily found homes in the grand halls of government and academia, and in the atriums of international hotels that were springing up all over post-World War II Japan.

Others like Shihoko Fukumoto sought to bridge the East and the West. Her entry into the 13th Biennial married indigo, through the ancient *shibori* dyeing process, with imagery that suggested a cross between the waves on an old kimono and the scallop forms of western quilts and embroidery.

Still others, led by Akio Hamatani, Masakazu and Naomi Kobayashi, Mihoko Matsumoto, Sachiko Morino, and Mariyo Yagi (all born in the 1940s) seemed intent upon creating work that was deeply rooted in a Japanese sense of beauty. These artists, among the first on the scene of the international fiber movement, prevailed. For just as Antoni Tàpies located in the ancient Romanesque civilization around him the essence of what it means to be Spanish, contemporary Japanese fiber artists ultimately shrugged off European influences and turned to their own culture to locate the wellsprings of what would become a new and glorious contemporary fiber movement. By 1995 when the last Lausanne biennial was held, Japanese artists had, one by one, journeyed home.

What does it mean to be Japanese in this new time? For Shihoko Fukumoto it meant to simplify, to pare down, to discard every unnecessary element of form. The scallops disappeared; the indigo and the *shibori* remain. Sometimes she used gold leaf, that sumptuous source of light glimmering through the darkness of old temples, to foil the inherent serenity of indigo-dyed cloth. Simple, simpler, and still simpler: by 2002 Fukumoto's work seems nothing less than shrouds for the gods.

This contemporary Japanese fiber movement, however, is not based in western minimalism. Repetitive? Yes, artists such as Hiroko Ohte create scale and grandeur by building a work with multiples of the same shapes and images. Spare? Yes, this art, however, is awash with elegance, brimming with sumptuousness, unsettled by underlying emotion. It is gorgeous, but subtly so. A cascading river of steel wire or an *Air Cube* of stainless steel filaments by Kyoko Kumai teems with the promise of sensual pleasure – even in this industrial age. Tetsuo Fujimoto sums up the opposing forces alive in Japanese fiber art when meditating on his own work: "It seems that dynamism and delicateness, flat plane and three-dimensional space, void and substance are now in and now out of sight in a sheet of cloth." This is not minimalism.

There are other defining forces. Jun Mitsuhashi, in his search to make art that was truly personal, chose light and space as the foundation for his work. His artistic concerns have evolved gradually from early, European-influenced, flatly-woven, brightly-colored wall hangings to the playful meditations on space that occupy him today. First he set weaving aside, exchanging the wall for three-dimensional space. Next he began to fabricate, to create within the environment. In 1993 he built a circle of houses from wood and felt, named *Watch for the Moon* – a title which may mean nothing at all. Over the decade, Mitsuhashi's art became lighter and more transparent; it now harbors only wisps of implied meaning. A *Moon Ship* might be a child's day dream. A *Floating Garden* is a three-dimensional Paul Klee. Mitsuhashi's pilgrimage echoes that of many a Japanese artist who passed through Lausanne over the years, in search of an art informed by the present-day international life but also deeply embedded in traditional Japan.

Hiroko Ohte
Close to Cloth '95-2

Whereas Issey Miyake and Rei Kawakubo fused East and West to create an aesthetic that transcends national identity, Hisako Sekijima took from the West the freedom to work outside the rigid confines of Japan's long basket tradition. She brings to her art the same aesthetic rigor found in historical Japanese basketry, the same spirit of modern-day experimentation, and the same need to be understood intuitively that underpins the contemporary Japanese fiber movement. Likewise, Reiko Sudo, schooled in industrial design and one of the great innovators in the design of mill cloth, is fiercely devoted to craftsmanship, to technical experimentation, and to beauty. Her amazing feat is to create exquisite, poetic cloth with rusty nails and techniques invented to paint cars and process milk.

To be a contemporary Japanese fiber artist is to think and work abstractly. Even when abstracted from something, the art remains abstract, just as the garments of the famous fashion designer Rei Kawakubo are reveries on the idea of clothing even more than clothing itself. In Noriko Narahira's *Scene of White*, clothing represents the human form although as clothing it is barely there, only deconstructed suggestions of human covering. And Suzumi Noda's wonderfully philosophical installations abstractly pose questions about the role of clothes, or words, or water. Among these artists, the imperceptible is a powerful presence.

As Koji Takaki says, "I desire to expose the invisible through my works. Invisibility infiltrates through the critical filter of skin; it exists as feelings like dry, cold and warm." Yuka Kawai reiterates, "The world reveals itself to us through both the visible and the invisible. The invisible is often more significant and provocative. . ."

Noriko Narahira

Sound of Nature (detail)

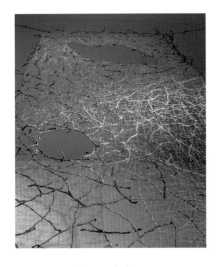

Kawai's monumental three-dimensional weavings are abstract contemplations on humanness. *Coexistence*, a fourteen-piece installation from 1993, and *Soothing Breath*, a two-piece installation from 1996, or *Encounter Yourself*, a room-size installation from 1998, suggest temporal states of being. Takaki's rooms of cotton cloth, whole or shredded back into threads, beckon the viewer into a place beyond ordinary experience. It is hard to imagine another movement within international contemporary art that is still so soundly ruled by abstraction.

Finally, although coming from one of the most populous islands on earth, this is an art that adores nature. Over and over these artists claim a deep kinship between their art and the natural world. Noriko Narahira says, "The main inspiration for my work has been my personal perception of nature. . . a strong sense of nature is imprinted on my mind." Kyoko Kumai says, "From my childhood I have liked the grass field blowing in the wind." And, "I have been making things to express earth, water, fire, wind and air." Takehiko Sanada, who makes his art from animal hair and fleece, states:

Takehiko Sanada
Listen / tell (detail)

The shape of life, which we are unable to sense or feel, may be different from that of the body inside which we dwell. That is to say that life may exist not in the inherent shape we possess, but in every single part, or form, in which a memory has been stored. And in that sense, a stranger's making of an object from parts of living creatures could be considered the creation of new life, because, at the time of its creation, the new object will bear a new memory shared with the stranger. Form stores memory, and life exists within it.

Just as Puritanism underpins the culture of the United States, Shintoism, the ancient and native religion of Japan which was primarily a system of nature and ancestor worship, may be at the core of the powerful connection to nature shared by these artists. When Tsuguo Yanai chose to explore the transience of life and time, it seemed natural for him to place objects made of hemp and stone in the forest to decompose naturally over a period of years. This bond with the natural world might also be the source of the high regard for craftsmanship and the sensitivity to materials that permeates this movement.

Light and shadow. Transparency and density. Space itself as a vital force. Utter spareness. Repetition. Materials drawn from both nature and industry. An intellectual search manifested visually in the arts. Rigorous craftsmanship based in both Japanese cultural history and present-day experimentation. An abiding tie to nature. These are the threads that run through the contemporary Japanese fiber movement. Through the hands of these artists, new art forms are emerging, rooted in a culture that spent centuries refining its sense of beauty. Contemporary fiber artists throughout Europe and the United States sought to be accepted in the larger art world. When Ann Hamilton crossed over to become an international star of installation art, when Anne Wilson was accepted into the 2002 Whitney Biennial in New York City with a conceptual installation of deconstructed lace, American fiber artists cheered. Whereas contemporary fiber artists in Japan sought instead to go deeper into the realm of Japanese art, which always included textiles. Ultimately they succeeded in creating an art movement that is radically their own.

Laurel Reuter
Director
North Dakota Museum of Art, USA

Artists

C
H
I
K
A

O
H
G
I

I am looking at the interface between
the space and the object.

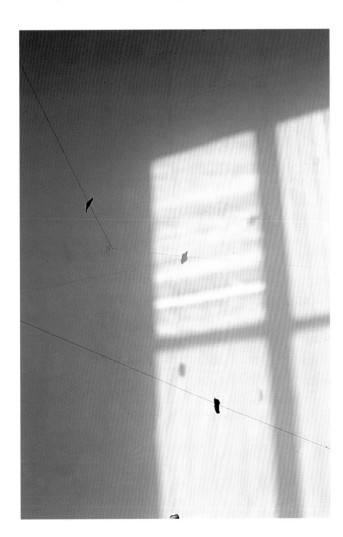

left:

Fragment
of Paper

1997

kozo, ganpi, pulp, cotton
thread, needle

right:

Fragment
of Sound

1998

charcoal, cotton thread

300 x 686 x 257cm

In my world elements such as trees and humans, light and shadow, or air and water, co-exist, none dominating the others. The seen and the felt are equals – nothingness has its own presence. As in music, the pauses, or spaces between, are as important as the notes or sounds.

Because I consider the space as important as my objects, I am interested in the edges of objects, whether cloth or paper. (I originally worked in cloth but have lately become more fascinated by paper, which I make myself by hand). Each object has a very subtle boundary between the space and itself. So the objects integrate themselves into the space. My installations are gradually revealed to the spectators by the passage of time.

Flickering shadows like drifting traces,

trembling as if to go out,

fragmented light animates the heavens.

right:
Fragmented Light (1997)
kozo, ganpi, cotton thread,
ramie thread, mirror
133 x 910 x 130cm

left:
Fragmented Light (2000)
sunlight, water, wind, mirror, cloth
195 x 92cm

I keep making, not knowing the consequences of my actions. The answer for my quest will only be revealed when it is installed in a space.

Filled with Light,

Water in the Air

1995

kozo, ganpi, cotton thread, ramie thread,

cypress board

380 x 1200 x 850cm

C H I K A

O H G I

Born   1960, Osaka

Education
1979-82   Post Graduate, Seian Women's College, Kyoto
1995-97   MFA, Seika University, Kyoto
1998   Artist-in-Residence, Canberra School of Art, ANU,
             Australia, supported by the Japan Foundation
1999   Artist-in-Residence, Rais Ark Museum of Art, Miyagi
2000   Research at Kyoto City University of Art
2001   Artist-in-Residence, Sainsbury Centre, Norwich, England (supported by the Japan Foundation)

Solo Exhibitions
1994   Wacoal Ginza Art Space, Tokyo
             Gallery Maronie, Kyoto
1995   Shoe Gallery Ota, Hyogo
1997   Gallery Suzuki, Kyoto
             X-port Tokyo
1998   Canberra Museum and Gallery, Australia
             Exhibition Space Tokyo International Forum, Tokyo
             Gallery Maronie, Kyoto
1999   Hirakata Municipal Gotenyama Art Centre, Osaka
             Exhibition Space Ecru + HM, Tokyo
             Higashiyama Youth Centre, Kyoto
2000   za Gallery, Kyoto
             Yatamo Plaza, Tokyo
2001   Gallery Ami and Gallery Kanoko, Osaka
             'ART SPACE LIFE blanc', Japan
2002   Gallery Maru Sankaku Shikaku, Kyoto

Selected Group Exhibitions
1987   'International Textile Competition '87 Kyoto', Kyoto International Conference Hall (also in '94, '97)
1992   '15th international Lausanne Biennial', Musée Cantonal des Beaux-Arts, Lausanne, Switzerland
1998   'Japanese Textile Miniature Exhibition Folding', Canberra Museum and Gallery, Australia (tour)
1999   'SOFA 1999 NYC', Seventh Regiment Armory, New York
2001   'Telos Textile Art Postcard Exhibition', Gallery Gallery EX, Kyoto
             'Textural Space' – Contemporary Japanese Textile Art, Farnham, England (tour)
2002   Paperworks 2002 INO, Paper Museum, Ino, Kochi

Stage of the Forest

1995

wood, silk thread, piano wire, silk organza

90 x 80 x 400cm

*J
U
N

M
I
T
S
U
H
A
S
H
I*

Today, instead of simply using cloth and paper, I use all kinds of materials such as wood, metal and stone.

Floating Garden

1998

brass wire, silk organza, stone

80 x 400 x 700cm

It is rare for my works to exude 'strength' . . .

Rather, they are ephemeral, soft, 'fragile' pieces . . .

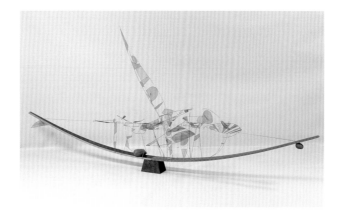

They encompass all that can be conveyed . . .

. . . through subtlety and delicacy.

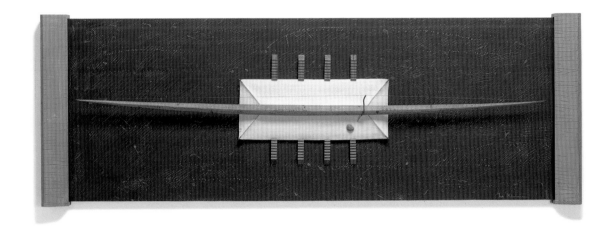

JUN MITSUHASHI

Perhaps my work is an extension of the modelling that I did when I was young. Originally I tried to express myself through dyeing and weaving, creating a flat picture, but I have moved gradually on to three-dimensional works as I have become more aware of the use of space.

top left:

Omen of Floating

1998

brass wire, feather,

silk organza

25 x 25 x 25cm

this page:

Bite at the Moon

1994

felt, wood, stone,

silk thread

60 x 10 x 180cm

centre left:

Moon Ship

1998

silk organza, wood, wire, stone,

brass wire

200 x 180 x 430cm

bottom left:

Waterscape (detail)

2000

wood, brass wire, seaweed

paper

360 x 30 x 2500cm

I regard my works as a small window allowing the viewer to take a look at phenomena such as omens of change and premonition.

J U N M I T S U H A S H I

Born   1954, Kyoto

Education and Awards
1998   Grand Prix, 4th "IN OUR HANDS" International Competition
1994   New Talent Prize, Kyoto Municipality
                Fine Art Award, 4th International Textile Competition '94, Kyoto
1990   Excellence Award, Selected Exhibition of Arts and Crafts, Kyoto
1989   Art and Culture Prize, 7th Kyoto Prefecture
1979-81   Kyoto City University of Arts (Post Graduate Course)
1975-79   Kyoto City University of Arts (Bachelor of Fine Art)

Selected exhibitions
1985, 86, 88, 89, 90, 91, 95, 98 Gallery Gallery, Kyoto (solo)
1987   Gallery TEMPORARY T&I, Kyoto (solo)
1988   ARCHI TEXTURE, Spiral Garden, Tokyo
1990   Gallery NAKAMURA, Kyoto (solo)
                SEIBU Art Gallery, Hyogo (solo)
1991   Perspectives from the Rim, Bellevue Art Museum, Seattle, USA
                Restress Shadows; Japanese Fibre Works, London, UK (tour)
1993   SIGA ANNUAL '93 - the Repro Action of Form, Museum of Modern Art Shiga
                Waves, Contemporary Japanese Fibre Work, Library and Gallery
                Ontario, Canada (tour)
1994, 2001   AD&A Gallery, Osaka (solo)
1994   Contemporary Textile Design – Dyeing, National Museum of Art, Osaka
2000   The Seaweed's Paper & 4 Artists, Rias Ark Museum of Art, Osaka
2001   Meeting Points, National Museum of Scotland, Edinburgh, UK
                Oriel 31 Davies Memorial Gallery, UK (solo)

Collections
                Kyoto Prefecture
                National Museum of Art, Osaka
                Rias Ark Museum of Art, Osaka
                Sumoto Municipal Health Centre
                Kumiyama Municipal Office

opposite:

Watch for the Moon

1993

wood, silk thread, felt

70 x 330 x 330cm

S
H
I
H
O
K
O

F
U
K
U
M
O
T
O

*My aim is to achieve an expressiveness within the
constraints of the clarity of the single indigo colour.*

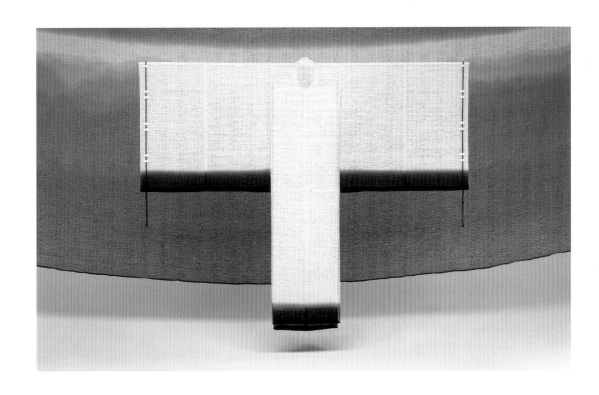

left:

HIKARI NO YUKUE

1993

indigo-dyed shihu-cloth, gold leaf

175 x 35cm

page 24:

JIKU-1

1991

indigo-dyed ramie

210 x 200cm

right:

Time Space 92-1 1992

indigo-dyed pineapple leaf fabric,

gold leaf

75 x 50cm

page 25:

Noh costume – KAICHO

(*The Tide of the Sea*) 2002

indigo-dyed pineapple-leaf fabric

173 x 222cm

First, there must be a new concept. The realization of originality involes ceaseless searching so that in an original work we find new and unique elements – new in idea, materials, techniques, tools or equipment. A new creative work can often be stimulated by the discovery of a technique. In *Meteor* we see a long thin white strip running through the centre of the deep indigo ground. This white line was born out of the creative use of a fibre-glass stick. A narrow length of *shihu* cloth woven from paper threads was hung from a U-shaped fibre-glass stick and then dyed in indigo. The fibre-glass leaves a white line in the dye which has a

tension, a sense of speed and a feeling of transparency; precisely what I was seeking.

My dyer's studio is equipped with many objects not generally associated with the craft. As well as glass fibre sticks, it has plastic indigo vats in specially ordered sizes, large individually made wooden tools around which cloth is wrapped in *shibori* dyeing, pulleys used for hanging heavy dye cloth for large works, plus specially equipped washing facilities and purified water etc. This collection of equipment resulted when trying to discover how to apply new ideas creatively.

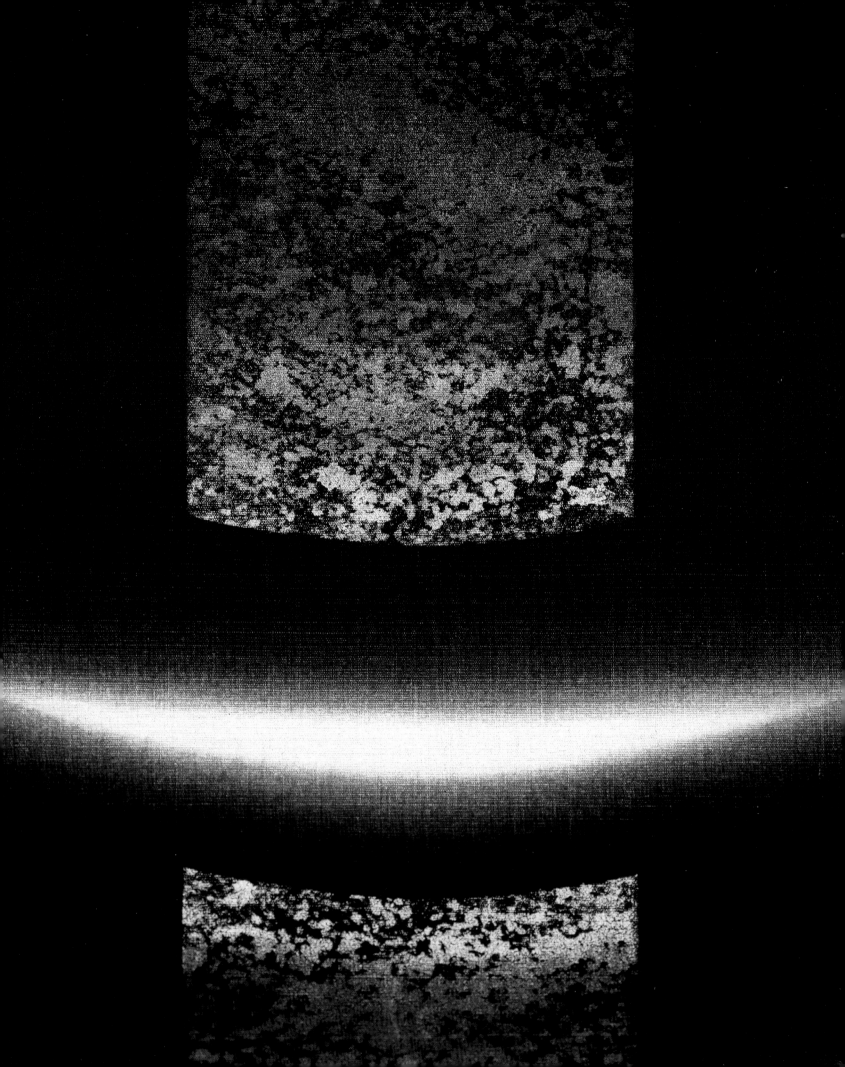

I hold simplicity as a firm principle in my work. To express an idea in a minimum of terms means a serious commitment to removing all extraneous elements: paring away and discarding all that is not essential in pursuit of clarity. Saying much in just a few words has been a strong expressive tendency in Japanese culture. My aim is to achieve an expressiveness that is profound within the constraints of the clarity and simplicity of the single indigo colour.

Finally, I believe that it is depth that is of the greatest importance in a true work. Depth means a penetration into the deep and fundamental nature of things. Depth is not just a matter of rational concept or idea, nor is it something one can always achieve through sheer commitment and devotion.

The Japanese word *oku* indicates an inner realm; maybe emphasis placed on inner depths – *oku* – is unique to Japan; however, I believe it is a universal value. The difficulty of expressing *oku* and any success in expression must surely be an intrinsic part of the artist's talent and temperament. I find it extremely difficult to realize, and have no clear idea of how to go about it. I do not know to what extent I achieve it.

OOUMI (The Sea)
1999
indigo-dyed ramie
160 x 155 x 70cm

S
H
I
H
O
K
O
F
U
K
U
M
O
T
O

Born   1945, Osaka

Education and Awards
1965-1968   BFA, Kyoto City University

Selected Solo Exhibitions
1990   Rösska Museet, Göteborg
1993   The Gallery at Takashimaya, New York, Tokyo, Kyoto
1996   The Tatsuno Museum of Art, Tatsuno
1999   Osaka Contemproary Art Center, Osaka
2001,1998, '95   Bellas Artes Gallery, Santa Fe, NM, USA
2002   Muromachi Muesum of Art, Kyoto

Selected Group Exhibitions
1986   Indigo: Natural Blue, Royal Tropen Museum, Amsterdam
1992,90,87   13th and 14th International Bienneal of Tapestry, and 15th
                 International Lausanne Biennial, Musée Cantonal des Beaux
                 Arts, Lausanne
1996   1st Flax and Linen Biennale in Upper Normandy, Rouen
1998   ASIAN AVANT-GARDE, Christies, London
1999   4ème Festival International de la Tapisserie, Beauvais
                 The Invitational Exhibition of Chongju International
                 Craft Biennale '99 Chongju
2001   Textural SPACE, Foyer Gallery and James Hockey Gallery, Surrey, UK (tour)
                 Crafts in Kyoto 1945-2000, The National Museum of Modern Art, Kyoto,
                 Contemporary Textile Weaving and Dyeing: Way of Formative Thinking,
                 The National Museum of Modern Art, Tokyo

Public Collections
                 The National Museum of Modern Art, Tokyo
                 The National Museum of Modern Art, Kyoto
                 The National Museum of Art, Osaka
                 Röhsska Museet, Göteborg
                 American Craft Museum, New York

TSUGUO YANAI

Often the true meaning and importance of something only begins to dawn on us when it is fading, decayed or lost to us for ever.

left:

Last Great Tree

1999

hemp, paper, dye, iron

400 x 200 x 200cm

Genius Loci 058

1992

hemp, lights

140 x 520 x 270cm

All matter erodes and fades away over time . . .

Stone Nest

1991-96

hemp, stone

top photo: 1991

middle photo: 1992

lower photo: 1994

approximate overall dimensions:

50 x 600 x 500cm

In 2000 I developed a series called Antiquities. In it, I sought to portray twenty important figures from the

20th century, giving them a weathered appearance. With the current speed at which information is conveyed,

I fear that these and other important figures and objects will fade from our memories if we do not find a way

to preserve them. By giving them this weathered appearance, it was my hope that their 'excavation' would

paradoxically rekindle memories of life from the suggestion of death.

above:

Antiquities

2000

hemp, paper, dye, wire, iron pedestals

160 x 50 x 50cm (20 pieces)

page 18:

Border: Connecting Passage

2002

hemp, soil, wood

250 x 480 x 460cm

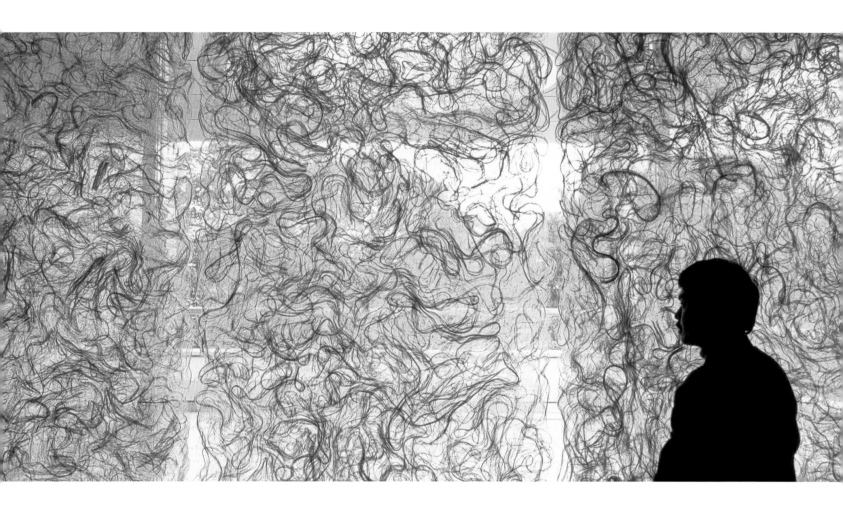

Following the terrorist attack of September 11th 2001, I began to think seriously of the meaning of borders: borders between Muslim countries and non-Muslim, between people of all races and religions, between parents and children, between friends and between lovers. In the tea room I designed *(illustration above)* I show the border between inside and outside; between Hagi where I was born and raised, and Tokyo where I have lived for 30 years. I brought soil from Tokyo to place inside the tea room, which is connected by a passageway or 'border' to Hagi on the outside, thereby altering the awareness of 'inside' and 'outside'.

T
S
U
G
U
O

Y
A
N
A
I

Born   1953, Hagi, Yamaguchi

Education and Awards
1977   Graduated Sokei Academy of Fine Arts (printmaking)
1978-80   Studied with Stanley W.Hayter at Atelier 17, Paris
1985   59th Kouten, Tokyo Metropolitan Museum, Osaka City Museum
               Aichi Museum, Nojima Prize
1990   18th Tokyo Biennale, Tokyo and Kyoto, Best Work Prize
               10th Paper Works of Contemporary Art, Fukui, Grand Prix

Selected Exhibitions
1985   17th Contemporary Art Exhibition of Japan, Tokyo Metropolitan Museum and
               Kyoto Municipal Museum
1985-90   Paper Works of Contemporary Art, Imadate, Fukui
1987   Function and Beauty of Japanese Paper, Yamanashi Prefectural Museum
1988   Paper and Contemporary Art, Galleria d'Arte Niccoli, Italy
1989   Contemporary Art Festival, Museum of Modern Art, Saitama
1990   18th Tokyo Biennale, Tokyo Metropolitan Museum and Kyoto Municipal Museum
1991   Frontiere de l'image, Espace Japon, France
1991-97   Summer Art Festival in Hakushu, Yamanashi
1993   Contemporary Japanese Paper Art, Maison de la Culture Cote-des-Neiges, Canada
               Asia-Pacific Triennial of Contemporary Art, Queensland Art Gallery, Australia
1994   Contemporary Japanese Paper Art, Hall of Awa Handmade Paper, Tokushima
               23rd Contemporary Art Exhibition of Japan, Tokyo Metropolitan Museum and
               Kyoto Municipal Museum
               JAPON-FRANCE Mixed Media Art Communication, Theatre X, Tokyo
1996   Statement Lying Behind Paper, Yamanashi Prefectural Museum of Art
1996-97   Nature-Material and Image, Artist House in Jerusalem, and Ein Harod Museum, Israel
1997   International Biennale of Prints, Yamanashi Prefectural Museum of Art
1999   Form of Japanese Paper, Nerima Art Museum, Tokyo
2000   Contemporary Paper Art, Imadate Art Hall, Fukui
               International Open-Air Fiber Art Exhibition, Issenba Park, Kamogawa, Chiba
2001   Fiber as Art, Gallery Space 21, Tokyo, and Sabae Contemporary Art Center, Fukui (tour)
2002   Border - Connecting Passage, Hagi Uragami Museum, Yamaguchi
               Wonderland of Paper, Gunma Museum of Art, Tatebayashi

GALLERY

K
O
J
I

T
A
K
A
K
I

My ambition is to expose the invisible through my works.

Invisibility infiltrates the skin; it exists in senses – dry, cold, warm.

Senses are clues to probe personal memories.

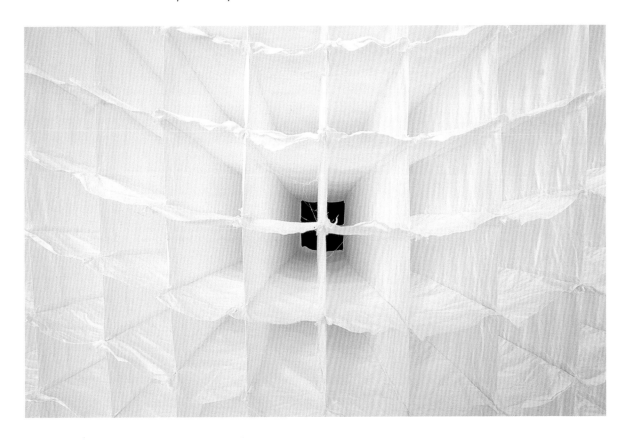

left:

Ma (1990)

cotton cloth, steel wire

400 x 30 x 220cm

above:

Ma (1994)

cotton cloth, steel pipe

150 x 150 x 220cm

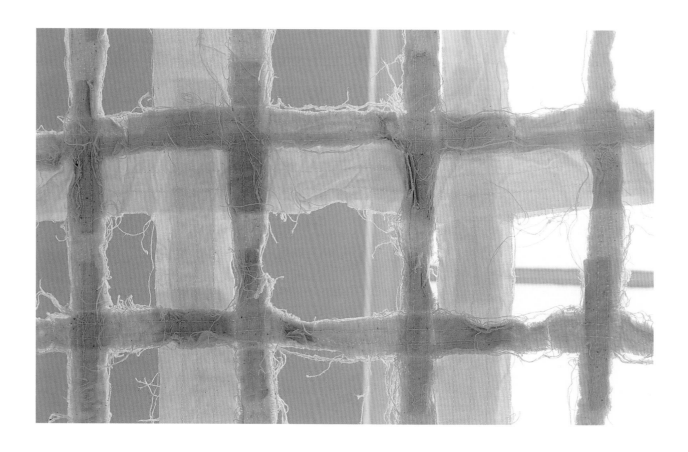

The spaces within my work offer the viewer a means of transmission to the spaces beyond the work.

Ma (2001)
cotton cloth
310 x 310cm

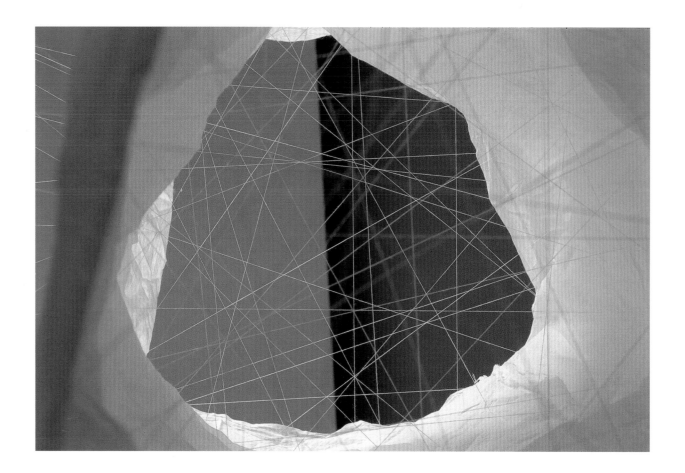

*Just as plant roots absorb water and the veins circulate water to every cell,
so the numerous spaces in my work are a passage for the senses from this
side to beyond. They are the entity between different planes.*

Ma (1996)
cotton cloth, cotton strings, steel pipe
60 x 100 x 60cm

K
O
J
I

T
A
K
A
K
I

Born   1954, Osaka

Education and Awards
1981   MFA from Kyoto City University of Arts

Selected Exhibitions
1985   The 12th International Lausanne Biennial, Switzerland
               Selected Art Exhibition, Kyoto Municipal Museum of Art
1986   Fabric and Thread in the Contemporary Art Scene, Spiral, Tokyo
1987   Needle Art, The Museum of Modern Art, Wakayama
1989   The 1st Perth International Craft Triennial, Western Australia
1990   Gallery Gallery, Kyoto (solo)
1991   Art Scene 1991– Each Material, Each Expression,
               The Tokusima Modern Art Museum
1993   Waves, Contemporary Japanese Fiberwork (tour, Canada)
1994   Light and Shadow - Japanese Artists in the Space, North Dakota
               Museum of Art, USA
               Gallery Gallery, Kyoto (solo)
1998   Kyoto Art Festival, Kikoku-tei, Kyoto
               Gallery Gallery, Kyoto (solo)
               IMAGINATIONS '98 Japanese Textile Miniature, Gasthuiskapel, Belgium
               Japanese Textile Miniature 'Folding', Canberra Museum and Gallery (tour)
1999   International Textile Competition Kyoto '99, The Museum of Kyoto
               Gallery Gallery, Kyoto (solo)
2000   Kimono as Canvas, Canberra Design Centre (tour)
2001   Textural Space, Contemporary Japanese Textile Art (tour)
               Gallery Gallery, Kyoto (solo)

*S
U
Z
U
M
I

N
O
D
A*

The red I use in my work signifies blood and the bonds between people. The three-dimensional frame signifies every possible blood-line drawn between people across the whole world.

left:

Red Frame (detail)

1999

plastic yarn, wood,

polyurethane foam, hand-made felt,

print, knit, paint

above:

Words possessing value as commodities: Water

2002

polyester cloth, paper, yarn, wood,metal

taps, plastic box, print, knit

The 'Diet Table' is far too narrow for a
p   i   z   z   a

Placed on it instead are calorie-free
w   o   r   d
d   o   u   g   h   n   u   t   s

What   does   it   mean   to   be
m e d i u m - s i z e d ?

What's   so   wrong   with   being
s   i   z   e - 1   8   ?

Our society, oversupplied with commodities,
cannot   cope   with   any   more,
but our appetites and brains are insatiable.

Words Possessing Value as Commodities: Diet

2002

cotton, polyester cloth, plastic yarn, wood, urethane

foam, spandex tape, print, knit

Born   1951, Osaka

Education and Awards
1970-1972   Osaka Designers' College, Interior Design major
1974   Kawashima Textile School
1985   Encouragement Award, Japan Crafts Competition, Asahi
1997   Fine Art Award, International Textile Competition, Kyoto

Solo Exhibitions
1986   Gallery Maronie, Kyoto, 1987, 90, 94, 95, 98, 2000
1989   Gallery Gallery, Kyoto, 1990, 95, 97, 2000, 02
1994 & 2000 Wacoal Ginza Art Space, Tokyo
2002   PlusMinus Gallery, Tokyo

Selected Group Exhibitions
1985   'Japan Crafts Competition', Asahi Contemporary Crafts
1988   'Archi-Texture Exhibition', Spiral Garden, Tokyo
1990   'KIRIN Contemporary Award', Kirin Plaza, Osaka
1992   'International Textile Contest', Hanae Mori Bl., Tokyo
             'Miniature Works', Gallery Gallery, Kyoto (tour: Belgium, Canada)
1993   'In Our Hands,' International Competition, Aichi.
1998, 2000   'International Textile Competition', Tokyo
1996   'KIRIN Contemporary Award Festival', Karin Plaza, Osaka
1997   'A Close Look at Miniatures', Musee de la Civilisation, Canada
1997, 99   'International Textile Competition', Kyoto
1998   'Viewpoint', Contemporary Art Center, Osaka
             'IMAGINATIONS '98', Gallery Gasthuiskapel, Belgium
             'Japanese Textile Miniatures', City Museum & Gallery, Canberra
             'Urban Heat Fashion Event', Moores Building, Perth
1999   'KIRIN Contemporary Award Senior 5', Kirin Plaza, Osaka
2001   'Contemporary Lace Exhibition', Powerhouse Museum, Sydney

S
U
Z
U
M
I

N
O
D
A

left:

Word Work Diet T-shirt

(detail)

2000

printed and knitted cotton cloth

right:

Table with a spinal cord F

1997

hand-made felt, plastic

140 x 200 x 1300cm

*H
I
S
A
K
O
S
E
K
I
J
I
M
A*

Baskets are interesting visually because of their containment of space.

left:

P-Y Move (detail)

1999

willow

31 x 25 x 25cm

above:

Difference

1997

willow

13 x 43 x 43cm

I spent the late 1970s in New York City, and was stimulated by the artistic trends emerging in the craft movement during that period.

A basket is a vessel full of space and shadows. I judge this space as a formal element of equal value to the physical material. I call it 'negative material', contrasting it with tangible materials of the basket's creation.

The mechanisms of structuring fiber materials always fascinated me. I divide basketry into six basic techniques: looped, knotted, coiled, plaited, weft-warped, and twined. Any basketry could be analyzed in terms of these. I call these universal physical rules 'basketry' constitution'. This 'constitution' has helped my basketry technically and aesthetically so much that I have used it extensively to abstract ideas for my creation. Conventional basketry,

however, could seriously restrict artistic freedoms. Through the ages the best materials, structural methods, and forms have been so honed, and basketry so highly developed that it works best to reproduce analogous forms.

Such objects inevitably convey the imageries of historic functions. These could easily eclipse any individualism. Here comes my challenge to reset the conventions in my own terms; to express myself.

I work with tree bark, branches, leaves, or the vines of various plants that I collect. They are not produced as craft materials.

They are far less standardised, less regular and less obedient. When I use them I cannot use conventional means to achieve the forms I intend. This forces me to review my expectations

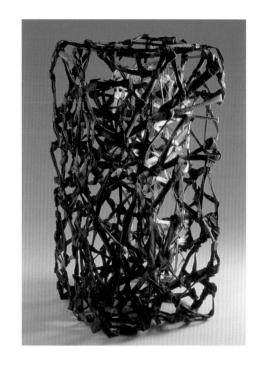

"400"
1994
walnut
20 x 36 x 31cm

from all angles. My basket-making is a product of these discoveries, and through it you can uncover my way of looking at things.

Interacted void

2001

walnut

20 x 24 x 24cm

Stuffed Volume

2002

walnut

18 x 21 x 21cm

Disturbed

1992

kudzu

11 x 57 x 39cm

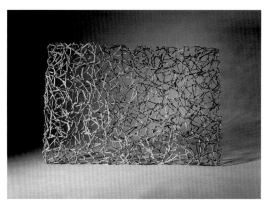

A Side to Side

2002

shuro palm, mulberry paper

21 x 31 x 27cm

H I S A K O   S E K I J I M A

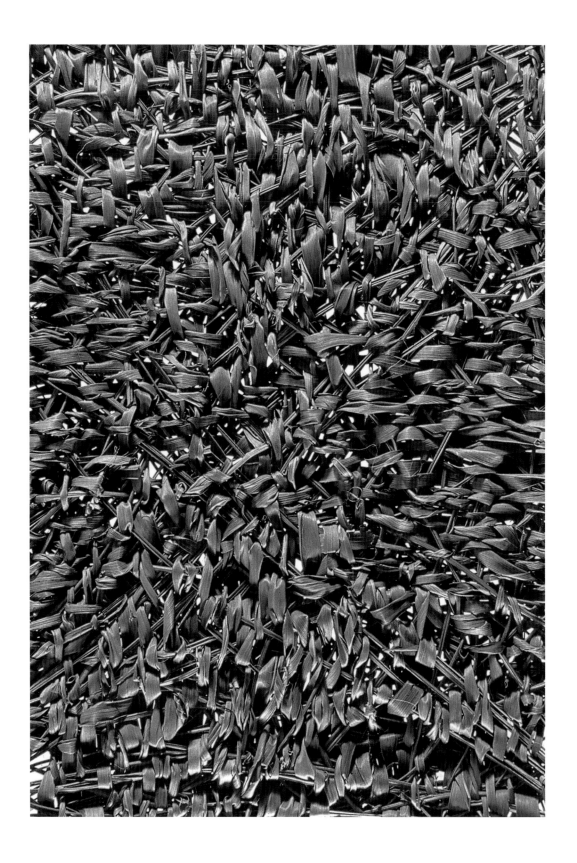

*H
I
S
A
K
O
S
E
K
I
J
I
M
A*

Born   1944, Tainan, Taiwan

Education and Professional
1966   BA in English Literature from Tsuda College, Tokyo
1986   Author of 'Basketry,' Kodansha International, Tokyo 1986

Solo Exhibitions
1985   Masuda Studio Gallery, Tokyo
1995   Gallery Isogaya, Tokyo
2000   Gallery Kandori, Tokyo
2002   'Basketry – Elegant Space', Exhibition Space,
               Tokyo International Forum, Tokyo

Selected Group Exhibition
1977   'Art of Basketry', Florence Duhl Gallery, New York
1989   'Tactile Vessel', Erie Museum, American Craft Museum, New York
1993   'Baskets: Redefining Volume and Meaning', Art Gallery, University of Hawaii, Manoa
1994   'The Domain of the Medium', Tokyo National Museum of Modern Art
1995   'Japanese Studio Crafts', Victoria & Albert Museum, London
1998   'Botanical Garden in Imagination', Hiratsuka City Art Museum, Hiratsuka
               'Nature as Object', The Art Gallery of Western Australia, Perth
               'Glen Kaufman and Hisako Sekijima', Brown Grotta Gallery, Wilton, CT, USA
1999   'Hi-Fiber…Weaving the World – Contemporary Art of Linear Construction',
               Yokohama Art Museum, Japan
               'International Contemporary Basketmaking', Crafts Council, London
2001   'Japan Under the Influence – Innovative Basketmakers Deconstruct Japanese Tradition',
               Brown Grotta Arts, Wilton, CT, USA
               'Flet-Braid', Nordyjlland Kkunstmuseum, Aalborg, Denmark
2002   'Survey Fiber 2002', Snyderman Works Gallery, Philadelphia, PA, USA

Collections
               The Art Gallery of Western Australia, Perth
               Tokyo National Museum of Modern Art
               Victoria & Albert Museum, London
               Erie Art Museum, Erie, Philadelphia

left:

Nine leaves (detail)

2002

shuro palm

4 x 38 x 39cm

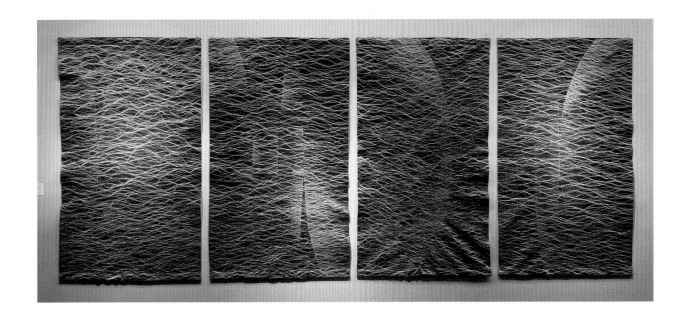

*T
E
T
S
U
O

F
U
J
I
M
O
T
O*

Vision is an important part of our daily recognition of things. But what we can recognize through vision is superficial. We can see a different world simply by changing our viewpoint.

left:
Work '99 - VII (detail)
1999
silk cloth, silk thread, sheer backing
(Pellon), natural plant dye
176 x 283 x 21cm

above:
Work '95 - IV
1995
hemp cloth, polyester thread, sheer
backing (Pellon), natural plant dye
82 x 434cm

It seems that dynamism and delicacy, flat plane and three dimensional space, void and substance are now in and now out of sight in a sheet of cloth. They appear as a dynamic picture surface from the distance of 50 feet, as an engulfing space from five feet, and as a delicate piling up of threads from five inches.

We can realize the presence of an invisible world in something by moving closer. I am now very interested in the fact that the universal macro world and the inner micro world seem to be alike. I try to make the macro and micro coexist in one picture through the lines of sewing; overlapping lines leading us to the inner world.

In December 1994 I exhibited the series *Machine Drawing*, I worked as if I were drawing pictures, but these pictures had to be recognised as a "sheet of cloth." I hope to express the wrinkles, distortions and drape of a sheet of cloth beautifully and naturally.

The micro-system of a single cell is the same as the system of the universe surrounding it, and I transfer such a system into a single sheet of cloth.

If we can say that in Western thought, we find essential value in the summit of everything. On the other hand, in Eastern thought, we find it in self-extinction. When I take away everything and I become one cell, I have the feeling that I can find a place of repose in a sheet of cloth and the feeling that I can absorb the system of the universe within myself.

Work '94-VII

1994

hemp cloth, silk thread, sheer backing (Pellon), natural plant dye

230 x 112cm (each piece)

T E T S U O   F U J I M O T O

Work '99 - I

1999

hemp cloth, polyester thread, sheer

backing (Pellon), natural plant dye

176 x 313 x 15cm

 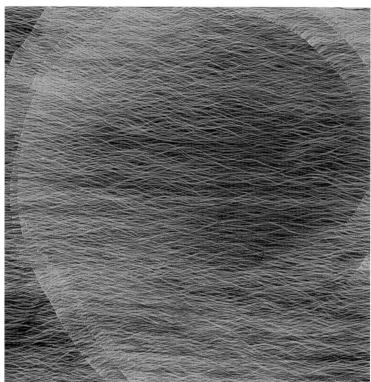

I can find a place of repose in a sheet of cloth

Work '97-XV

1997

hemp cloth, polyester thread, sheer backing
(Pellon), natural plant dye

62 x 63cm

Work'97-VIII

1997

hemp cloth, polyester thread, sheer
backing (Pellon), natural plant dye

202 x 245cm

T
E
T
S
U
O

F
U
J
I
M
O
T
O

Born   1952, Kyoto

Education and Awards
1977   BA, Kyoto City University of Arts (dyeing and weaving)
1979   Postgraduate Program, Kyoto City University of Arts,
            (dyeing and weaving)
1984   Mayor's Prize, 36th Kyoten
1992   Fulbright Grant; Fulbright Artist / Scholar in Residence 92-93
1994   Special Superior Prize, Kyoto Art and Crafts Biennale
1999   Grand Prix, ITF 6th International Textile Competition, Kyoto
1999   Kyoten Prize, Kyoten

Selected Exhibitions
1984   'Moderne Textilkunst aus Japan Tapisserien und
            Textilobjekte', Museum Bellerive, Zurich
            Museum of Decorative Art, Lausanne
            Nederlands Textielmuseum, The Netherlands
1987   '13th International Biennial of Tapestry'
            Cantonal Museum of Fine Arts, Lausanne,
1991   'Kyoto Fibers', Montclair State University, NJ, USA (tour)
1992   '15th International Lausanne Biennial'
            Museum of Fine Arts, Lausanne,
1997   'The Contemporary Stitch: JAPAN STYLE', Art Gallery
            Montclair State University, NJ; SIUC University Museum
            Southern Illinois University, IL, USA (tour)
2001   'Textural Space', Foyer Gallery and James Hockney Gallery
            The Surrey Institute of Art and Design,
            University College of Farnham, UK (tour)
            'Crafts in Kyoto 1945-2000',
            National Museum of Modern Art, Kyoto,
            The National Museum of Modern Art, Tokyo
2002   '5th International Festival of Tapestry and Fiber Art'
            Musee Departmental, Beauvais, France

*H
I
R
O
K
O

O
H
T
E*

I have always been conscious of the vagueness and ambiguity of cloth whose existence is necessarily dependent on its relationship with something else.

left:

Close to Cloth '95-2

1995

cotton, jute

13 x 50 x 50cm

(20 pieces)

right:

Store or Seal – Izumi Murota

2001

paper yarn, ramie, printed cloth

20 x 20cm

It is weaving technique which attracts me to work in this form. I consider only three weaving techniques are suited to creating patterns on cloth freely – tapestry, ikat, and double or triple weaving. But I seek expressions unique to weaving, created by warp and weft, I seek original woven expressions for which tapestry is unsuited.

Initially, I created many one-dimensional works, in which the main theme of the production was to simplify and create a motif by using ikat and a great variety of color. My intention was to give a sense of dimensions to a thin cloth and create a visually textural effect.

In the course of my efforts, my focus has shifted to the cloth itself. In particular, by using double weaving, I examine the fact that the cloth has two surfaces. In this process, I found the cloth to have developed an expression deeply concerned with space. My attention was drawn to the great diversity of the cloth.

Recent works present the cloth's function of 'creating a situation' setting up woven clothes in a space, connecting the cloth and space closely, and thus involving people. I have been seeking to highlight positive features of fabric; such work originates in my quest for new forms linked to clothing.

left:

Close to Cloth '95-1

1995

cotton, jute

300 x 32 x 32cm

above:

Interior

1997

cotton, jute

room size installation

*H
I
R
O
K
O*

*O
H
T
E*

Born   1960, Japan

Education and Awards
1983   BA from Kobe University
1984   Prize of Encouragement, Kyoto Art and Crafts Exhibition
1985   Graduated, Kawashima Textile School
1987   2nd prize, Asahi Contemporary Crafts Competition
1992   1st Prize, Kyoto Art and Crafts Exhibition
2001   Silver prize, 10th International Triennial of Tapestry, Lodz, Poland

Selected Exhibitions
1985   'Exhibition of Arts and Crafts' by Selected Artists,
             Kyoto Prefectural Center for Art and Culture
1987, 97   'ITF International Textile Competition', Kyoto
1988, 89, 93, 98   Gallery Maronie, Kyoto (solo)
1989   Gallery Muu, Kyoto (solo)
1990, 93, 98   Wacoal Ginza Art Space, Tokyo (solo)
1991, 92, 95, 97, 2000 Gallery Gallery, Kyoto (solo)
1992, 95   'Miniature Works 18 x 18', Gallery Gallery, Kyoto
1993   Shiga Annual, 'Fiber-Work/ the Repro-Action of Form',
             Museum of Modern Art, Shiga
1996   Art Space Niji, Kyoto (solo)
1998   'Imaginations', Contemporary Japanese Textiles Exhibition,
             Gallery de Qeeste, Loker, Belgium
1999   Art Life Mitsuhashi, Kyoto (solo)
             'Fiber As Art VIII '99', Gallery Space 21, Tokyo
2000   'Fiber As Art IX', Gallery Space 21, Tokyo
             'Folding-Exchange – Exhibition of Works in Fiber', Craft Center, Itami
2001   'Meeting Points', National Museum of Scotland, Edinburgh
             Gallery Gallery, Kyoto (solo)

Collections
             Kyoto Prefecture
             The Museum of Modern Art, Shiga

left:

Wall for Going Through

2000

silk, pineapple yarn, paper yarn

300 x 300 x 300cm

S
A
N
A
D
A

T
A
K
E
H
I
K
O

My works embody my memories, experiences and internal conflicts; and can be worn like garments or placed on display.

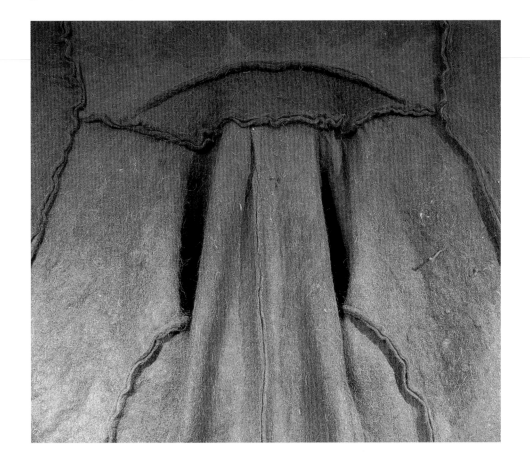

left:

From Top to Bottom
1999 (detail of reverse view)
animal hair, fleece
300 x 60 x 560cm

above:

Listen / tell (detail)
1998
animal hair, fleece
360 x 60 x 560cm

My creative activities began with my experiences travelling in my twenties.

Life continually gathers memories that are unchanging despite the changes that life brings to the body and its environment.

Life may exist not in our inherent shape, but in every form in which a memory has been stored. In that sense, a stranger making an object from leather, part of a living creature, could be considered to be creating new life. At the time of its creation, the new object will bear a new memory shared with the stranger. Form stores memory, and life exists within it, so new form stores new memory and, arguably, new life exists within this new form.

I spin yarn from sheep's wool, animal hair or raw plant fibre to make felt. Through this process, I work on making the intangible language tangible in me. In other words, I embody my memories, experiences and internal conflicts in my works, which can be worn like a garment, at times, or be placed on display as an object.

When we eliminate the 'edge' or *kiwa* – physical body and skin – that envelops a human life, and when the barrier separating the interior and exterior of the body disappears, the indwelling essence of life is released to the ouside. The physical interior and exterior vanish, providing us with a further space or place to exist. As long and as far as such a space or place extends, the essence of life will live on.

The *kiwa* that bounds the essence of life cannot be verified, in terms of consciousness or the senses, and the essence of life exists somewhere beyond the ego, or perceivable self and the non-ego or imperceptible not-self. That is to say, the *kiwa* is a mere concept we humans have invented, and our intrinsic essence of life exists apart from our physical and conscious senses. After all, the *kiwa* is a one-sided topological surface having no interior or exterior, and the essence of life exists only in a place that transcends the physical interior or exterior.

I pursue my works with a focus on life and existence. To verify my existence, I look for clues in what is within my body, enveloped in its integument. Yet this is not a clue to life itself. How much, after all, can we understand about the physical bodies that we call

'ourselves'? Though we try, through sight, hearing, touch, smell, and taste, to unravel everything about our existence, no clue pointing to the essence of our being can we find.

left:
Hand in Hand
(detail)
1998
animal hair, fleece
330 x 90 x 550cm

right:
From the Left into the Right
1997
fleece
10,000 x 3 x 90cm

When the barrier separating the interior and exterior of the body disappears, the indwelling essence of life is released to the outside.

There is no Upper or Lower Space
2002
animal hair, fleece
540 x 21 x 340cm

S
A
N
A
D
A

T
A
K
E
H
I
K
O

Born   1962, Tokyo

Education and Awards
1881-84   Studied at Kuwasawa Design School
1984-85   Postgraduate course at Kuwasawa Design School
1985-92   Worked for Issey Miyake, Inc
1994   Assistant to sculptor Richard Deacon,England
2001-   Associate Professor at the Joshibi University of Art and Design, Tokyo

Selected Exhibitions
1995   Partnership work 'Them and Us', Lisson Gallery, London
              The 31st Asian Modern Art Exhibition, Tokyo and Shanghai, China
1996   'Now and Then', Gallery Yamaguchi, Tokyo (solo)
1997   'Memory', Design Gallery, Tokyo (solo)
1998   'Between Body and Life', Tokyo International Forum Exhibition Space (solo)
              'Inside for Outside', Marzee Gallery, The Netherlands
              Designed costumes for Miyamoto Amon's dance performance, Art Sphere, Tokyo
1999   'Arai Junichi/ Sanada Takehiko' Exhibition, Yurinkan, Gumma, Japan
              'Impact 3', Gallery Tokyo Humanite, Tokyo
              'Personal Architecture', Design Gallery, Tokyo (solo)
2000   'Living in Fibre', Tokyo International Forum Exhibition Space, Tokyo (solo)
              Workshop 'Five Senses', The Hiratsuka Museum of Art, Kanagawa
              'Wool in Wool', The Koiwai Farm, Iwate, Japan (solo)
2001   'Project in the Field', The Koiwai Farm, Iwate (solo)
              'E12' Tokyo, Japan (tour to Vancouver, Montreal, Halifax)
2002   'Break the Seal', Gallery Tokyo Humanite, Tokyo (solo)
              Exhibition of Contemporary Art of Portugal and Japan
              Saga-cho Exhibition Space, Tokyo (solo)

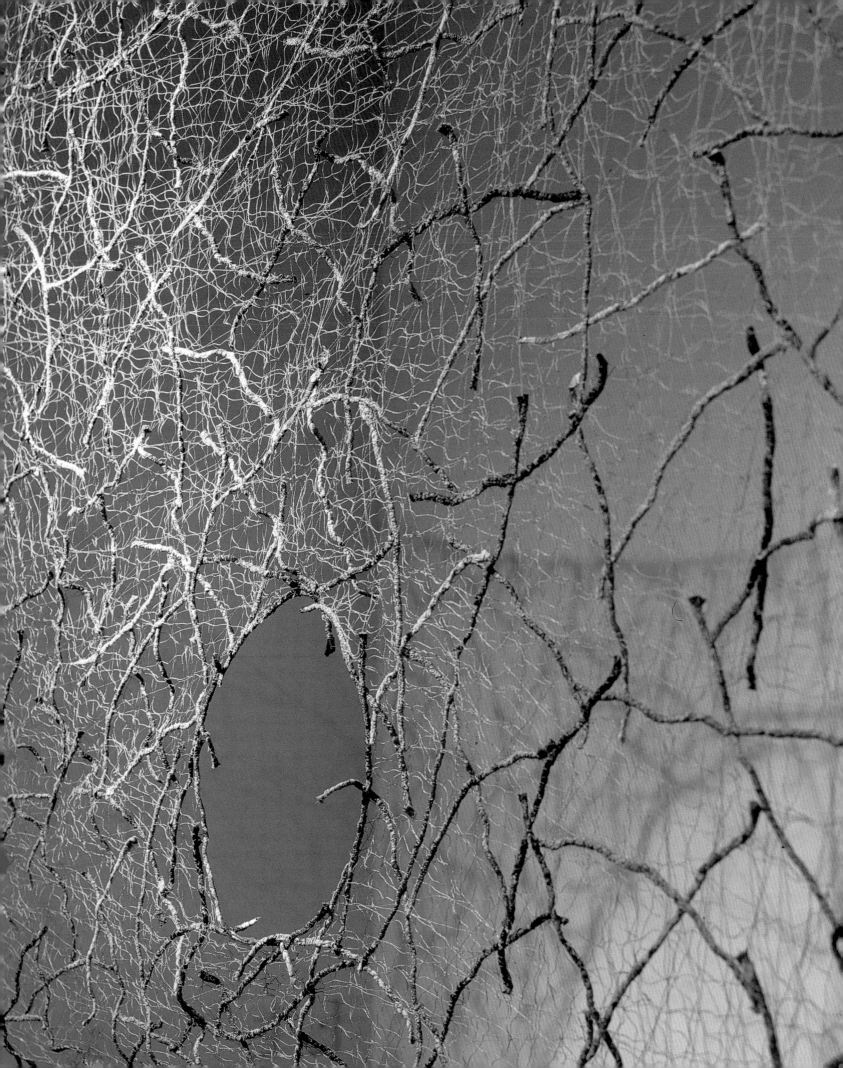

N O R I K O   N A R A H I R A

I am fascinated by nature; and my work as a lace-maker posed me a challenge early on in my career: in a country with no tradition of lace-making, how to express my vision of nature, and be true to my technical development whilst remaining firmly within my own Japanese heritage.

left:

Sound of Nature (detail)

1994

printed cotton, polyester thread

160 x 360cm

above:

Sound of Nature (installation)

1994

printed cotton, organza,

polyester thread

Scene of White
1999
felt, organza, polyester mesh,
polyester thread
each dress life-size

opposite: detail

My perception of nature has been the main inspiration for my work. When I was an art student, I lived close to nature. I became aware of its power, the texture of its creatures, its smell and sound, the feeling of air and water. The source of my work lies in these experiences.

Much of my early work was in lace. There is no tradition of lace-making in Japan, but my perspective is Japanese, so I wanted to bring this to my work with lace. I found many ideas among Japanese traditional patterns and colors. In Japan, we have a tradition of using multiple prints – print on print on print, and strongly contrasting colors exemplified in the *kimono* and *obi*.

Recently, I have been exploring white. White surfaces reflect light and shadow and are sensitive to colors. White has so much power, and textiles provide such variety of texture, that white becomes a huge color field. The challenge is to express color images in a white creation. The images will change with the light over the course of a day. So, the color and surface of white objects will be changed by daylight.

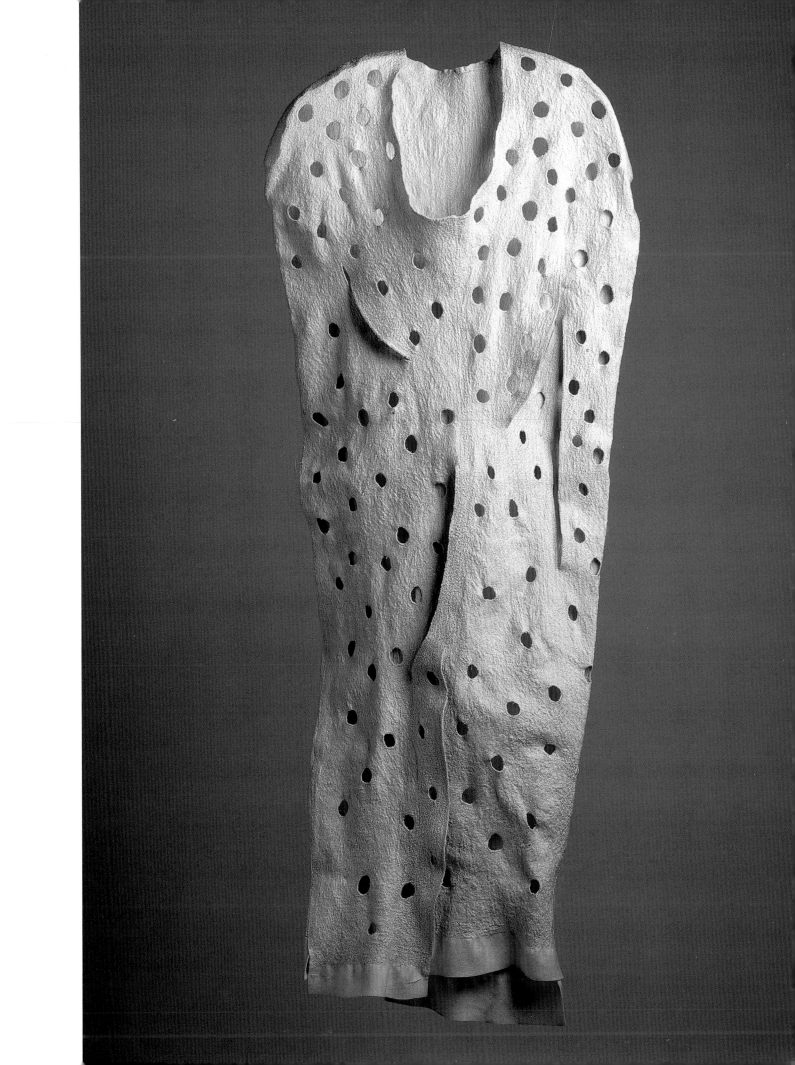

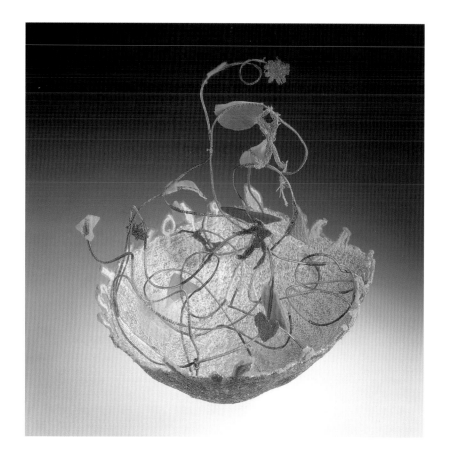

I love working in miniature – a fictional world held inside an imaginary space.

What a Fine Day!
2000
felt, organza, gut,
polyester thread
25 x 20 x 20cm

N
O
R
I
K
O

N
A
R
A
H
I
R
A

Born   1948, Hiroshima

Education and Awards
1967-1971   Bachelor of Fine Arts, Kyoto City University of Art
1971-1973   Post Graduate, Kyoto City University of Art
1994   Golden Bobbin Prize,
                6th International Lace Biennial
1995   Rise Nagin Jury Prize,
                Fiberart International '95
1996   Golden Bobbin Prize,
                 7th International Lace Biennial
1998   'International Lace for Fashion Award',
                Powerhouse Museum, Sydney

Solo Exhibitions
1980   Gallery Maronie, Kyoto, 1984, 86, 91, 92, 94, 96, 98
1999, 2002   Gallery Gallery, Kyoto
2000   Gallery Nishikawa, Kyoto

Selected Group Exhibitions
1991   'In Our Hands', an International Competition,
                 Nagoya Trade & Industry Center, Aichi, Japan, 1993, 95, 2000
                'Betonac International Competition', St. Stuiden, Belgium, 2000
1992   'Textile Miniature Works', Contemporary Art of Japan,
                 Gallery Gallery, Kyoto, tour to Belgium, Canada, Australia
                'International Biennial of Miniature Textiles', Szombathely, Hungary, 1994
1994   'International Lace Biennial', Brussels, Belgium 1996, 98
1995   'Fiberart International', Pittsburgh, USA 1997
1998   'Imaginations '98', Contemporary Japanese Textile, Wit Blad, Watou, Belgium
                'Imaginations '98', Japanese Textile Miniatures, Gasthuischapel, Popringe, Belgium
                'Japanese Textile Miniature – Folding', Canberra Museum & Gallery (tour)
2000   'Embroidery 2000', GalleryMateria, Arizona, USA
                'Folding – an Exhibition of works in Fiber', Itami Craft Center, Hyogo, Japan
                Powerhouse Museum, Sydney
2001   'Meeting Points – New Works in Fiber', Japan and Scotland
                'Fiber Connections', Edinburgh College of Art, Edinburgh

Collections
                St Gallen Textile Museum, Switzerland
                Lace & Costume Museum, Belgium

Y
U
K
A

K
A
W
A
I

The world reveals itself to me both through the visible and the invisible. The invisible is often more significant and provocative, creating within me unlimited images.

left:

Soothing Breath
(detail)
1996
hemp, stainless steel
240 x 120 x 120cm
(2 pieces)

right:
Far Voice (detail)
1994
rayon, stainless steel
230 x 30 x 25cm
(18 pieces)

I trained in textiles, specialising in weaving, where various rules intrinsic to hand weaving have helped me to attain clarity from chaos. These rules transform threads into woven works, involving repetitive action, like the action of waves rolling in, and painstaking effort, as if piling up heaps of stones.

This process serves as a stark contrast to my busy life in Tokyo. My weaving is a solitary effort, and when working, I become absorbed in the somatic action. My clumsy hands become attuned to the touch and the behavior of the materials, and the technique becomes a tactile, visual language. Dyeing the warp and the weft, planning the weaving structures, colors and textures, all become the skin of my work. Even simple techniques such as folding, twisting, swelling and hanging, serve to bridge the gap between woven material and sculptural organic form.

Creativity is for me a process of exploring the invisible, knowing the external world, and finding self-understanding. The initial step must be born of an inner spontaneous urge. I try to avoid becoming overly captivated by technique and craftsmanship because it can disturb the process. At the same time I am very aware that the intelligence of the hands is indispensible in the process of my work. I feel a tension between my desire to explore the wonder that lies outside the realms of intellect, and the material craft of my work.

The solidity of the loom makes me feel ambivalent: it brings serenity, but sometimes also a disquieting irritation.

I am drawn to spaces that evoke a certain physical or emotional state. I am interested in how art works are situated in space and how this can create an experience that stimulates all the senses. I believe the artistic experience can go beyond language and even cross cultural barriers.

this page and opposite:
Untitled
1999
cloth, felt, cane,
cotton, wax

YUKA KAWAI

I feel a tension between my desire to explore the wonder that lies outside the realms of intellect, and the material craft of my work.

I am interested in how art works are situated in space and how this can create an experience that stimulates all the senses.

Untitled
1999
plant stalk, cotton

Y
U
K
A

K
A
W
A
I

Born   1963, Tokyo

Education and Awards
1986   BFA, Tama Art University, Tokyo
1988   MA, Tama Art University, Tokyo
1991   MFA, University of Washington, Seattle, WA
1998   Japanese Government Overseas Study Program
1999   POLA Art Foundation Overseas Research Program for Artists
1998-2000   Goldsmiths College, University of London

Selected Exhibitions
1992   Gallery Kobayashi, Tokyo (solo)
1993   Gallery Kobayashi, Tokyo (solo)
              'The Suntory Prize '92', Suntory Museum of Art, Tokyo
              Sembikiya Gallery, Tokyo (solo)
1994   Gallery Kobayashi, Tokyo (solo)
1995   '8th International Triennial of Tapestry', Central Museum of Textiles, Lodz, Poland
              'Contemporary Direction in Japanese Fibre Art', Kyoto Municipal Gallery
1996   Gallery Kobayashi, Tokyo (solo)
1997   'Anticipation of Beauty', Takashimaya Art Gallery, Tokyo
              (tour: Yokohama, Kyoto and Osaka)
1998   Gallery Kobayashi, Tokyo (solo)
1999   'The Invisible Exhibition' Pezinok Central Park, Pezinok, Slovak Republic
2001   'Contemporary Textiles Weaving and Dyeing: Ways of Formative Thinking',
              Crafts Gallery, The National Museum of Modern Art, Tokyo

Professional
1992-98, 2000-01   Tokyo Kasei University, Tokyo
1997-98, 2000-02   Tokyo National University of Fine Arts and Music, Faculty of Fine Arts
2001-present   Tama Art University, Tokyo

Textiles are not just a pleasure to look at, they are a marvel to be experienced with all five senses: the feel of textiles in the hand or on the body, the periodic rustling sounds, even the taste on the lips.

right:

Origami Pleat

1997

polyester

left:

Paper Roll

2002

nylon

When designing textiles, I am strongly aware of two things. One is the texture and how the finished fabric will feel to the fingertips – crisp or slick or rough or coarse. These sensations are, to me, the very essence of expression in textiles, and so largely define how I go about designing.

The other important thing I bear in mind is not to make a 'front' or 'back'. Often people ask me 'which is the right way up'. This is probably because I make no clear distinction myself when designing. Nor do I design fabrics for a particular purpose. This is perhaps because I want our fabrics to be enjoyed as fabrics, not for any special use. Only when cut or sewn do they take on a clear 'inside' and 'outside'. This is a basic principle of my design work.

Burner Dye

2000

stainless steel

Cavern

1997

cotton 70%, rayon 30%

Website

hand-beaten, felted

1995

R
E
I
K
O

S
U
D
O

Born   1953, Niihari, Ibaraki

Professional Career

1975-77	Assistant to Prof. Hideho Tanaka, Faculty of Textiles, Musashino Art University, Tokyo
1977-84	Freelance Textile designer with Kanebo, Nishiwaka and others
1984 - 89	Textile Designer, NUNO Corporation
1989-	Director, NUNO Corporation Lecturer, Faculty of Textiles, Musashino Art University, Tokyo Zokei University

Selected Exhibitions

1994	'2010 – Textiles and New Technology,' Crafts Council, London 'Japanese Design – a survey since 1950,' Philadelphia Museum of Art 'Runway Show of Japanese Fashion,' North Dakota Museum of Art
1995	'NUNO: Japanese Textiles for the Body' University of Oregon Museum of Art
1996	'Textile Magicians,' The Isreal Museum of Modern Art
1998	'Structure and Surface: Contemporary Japanese Textiles' The Museum of Modern Art, New York
1999	'Structure and Surface: Contemporary Japanese Textiles' The Saint Louis Art Museum
2000	'NUNO: Contemporary Japanese Textiles', Anna Leonowens Gallery Nova Scotia College of Art and Design 'Structure and Surface: Contemporary Japanese Textiles', San Francisco, Museum of Modern Art (tour, Germany)

Permanent Collections

Cooper Hewitt Museum
Museum of Art, Rhode Island School of Design, Providence
Musée des Arts Décoratifs de Montréal
Museum of Applied Arts, Helsinki
The Saint Louis Art Museum
Philadelphia Museum of Art
Museum of Fine Arts, Boston
Victoria & Albert Museum, London
The Metropolitan Museum of Art
The Museum of Fine Arts, Houston
The Museum of Modern Art, New York

*K
Y
O
K
O

K
U
M
A
I*

I have been making things that I myself hope to see and have never seen before.

left:

Flame

1990

stainless steel filaments

300 x 70 x 1000cm

above:

Blowing in the Wind

1988

stainless steel filaments

20 x 20 x 20cm

Since childhood I have been interested in fabrics filled with wind such as sails, flags, washing blowing in the breeze, carp streamers and in fields of grass blowing in the wind.

In 1969 I began weaving using wool, cotton, linen, and silk. I started to use stainless steel filaments in 1975 to express the curves of various fabrics. Using stainless steel filaments for the warp and the weft, these images led me to make curved fabrics.

The thin pieces of stainless steel filament mass-produced in a factory are not only inorganic but also monotonous by themselves. Even so, when woven, twisted or bundled together they take on an organic appearance that expresses aspects of wind, air, and light.

I always aim at making my works appear to hover, breathing and existing in mid-air, not something which stands out as a solid work formed of hard materials.

These days I enjoy the profound beauties of the grass field in the desolate season of winter. I am stimulated to express these images in my work over and over again.

Air
1988
stainless steel filaments
250 x 1000 x 400cm

above:

Blowing in the Wind

1985-87

stainless steel filaments, cotton threads

230 x 30 x 1000cm

Born   1943, Tokyo

Education and Awards
1962 -66   Tokyo National University of Fine Arts & Music
1975   New Talent Prize, Japan Craft Design Exhibition
1983   Excellence Prize, Japan Craft Design Exhibition
1987   New Technology and Kyoto Governor's Prize;
                  1st International Textile Competition
1998   Bronze Medal: 9th International Tapestry Triennial,
                  Lodz, Poland

Solo Exhibitions
1991   Museum of Modern Art, New York
1983-2002   Twenty five solo shows in Japan & abroad

Selected Group Exhibitions
1987   13th Lausanne International Tapestry Biennial, Switzerland
1987   1st, 2nd, 3rd, 5th International Textile Competition,
                  Kyoto, 6th Juror
1994-97   'Textiles and New Technology 2010', UK (tour: The Netherlands)
1995   'Japanese Fiber Arts', Victoria and Albert Museum London
1997-02   'Challenge of Materials', Science Museum, London
1998   9th International Tapestry Triennial, Lodz, Poland, 10th Juror
1999   'Contemporary Art of Linear Construction' Yokohama Museum of Art, Japan
2000   '1st Echigo Tsumari Art Triennial', Niigata, Japan
2001   'Textural Space',UK (tour)

Work in Collection
                  Savaria Museum, Hungary
                  Musée des Arts Décoratifs de Montréal, Canada
                  Museum of Modern Art, New York, USA
                  Ohita Prefectural Art Museum, Japan
                  Victoria & Albert Museum, London, UK
                  Ashikaga City Art Museum, Japan
                  Science Museum, London, UK
                  Lodz Central Museum of Textiles, Poland
                  Ohita City Art Museum, Japan
                  Gunma Prefectural Museum of Modern Art, Japan
                  Musée de Textiles, Angers, France

K
Y
O
K
O

K
U
M
A
I

Air Cube

1996

stainless steel filaments

120 x 150 x 150cm

© **Telos Art Publishing**
PO Box 125, Winchester
England SO23 7UJ
www.telos.net
sales@telos.net
editorial@telos.net

Authors: Laurel Reuter and Keiko Kawashima
Editor: Matthew Koumis
Co-Editor and Consultant: Keiko Kawashima
Sub-Editor: Mary-Rose Tatham
Graphic Designer: Rachael Dadd
Reprographics: Anorax Ltd, Leeds
Print: Offset Colour Print Ltd, Southampton.

ISBN 1 902015 02 9

A CIP catalogue record for this book is available from the British Library.

Notes: all dimensions are shown in metric, height x width (x depth where appropriate).
Artists' biographies included within this volume have been edited to a consistent length.

Photo credits:

Yoshimitsu Baba, Kazuo Fukunaga, Takashi Hatekeyama, Seiryu Kai, Junichi Kanzaki, Robo Kocan,
Akira Koike, You. Kobayashi, Sue McNab, K. Nakano, Koichi Nishimura, Mitsuto Saitó, Taku Saiki,
T. Sakurai, Mareo Suemasa, Y. Takayama, K. Ushiro, Kemji Yamazaki, Masanobu Yamada, Makoto Yano.

Editor's Acknowledgements:

I would like to express my sincere thanks to all the artists and contributors to this book, and in
particular to Keiko Kawashima for her invaluable help throughout. Any errors remain squarely my own.
Thanks also to Shirley Channon for translating the introduction; to Diane Neptune, Sara Lordi Marker,
Kaeko Nakagawa, Freya, Colin, and Cesar for assistance. Last but not least, to Poppy, Tamsin and Maia:
thank you for your patience! MK